Talk Less, Listen More
The Power of Silence in Effective Communication

Table of Contents

We have two ears and one mouth so that we can listen twice as much as we speak.

— Epictetus

Chapter 1. Introduction

Unleash the magnetic pull of your words through the potent art of silent communication! In our thrilling Special Report titled "Talk Less, Listen More: The Power of Silence in Effective Communication", we delve deep into the hidden strengths of quietude and the profound effect it can have on your personal and professional interactions. With our engaging discussions, backed by compelling research and captivating anecdotes, you'll learn not only to harness the power of silence but also to master the subtle intricacies of dynamic dialogue. This enlightening journey offers a fresh perspective and equips you to become an extraordinary communicator. Sit back, devour every page, and let your communication skills get transformed from ordinary to extraordinary! Your voyage towards becoming a more powerful and persuasive communicator starts here. Buy this Special Report now and embark on an extraordinary journey towards more enriching and satisfying communication experiences.

Chapter 2. The Artful Science of Silence

We embark on this journey towards understanding the art of silence with due reverence to the influential power it possesses. Recalling from our shared common narratives and vivid imagery of verbose speakers, resounding with prolific streams of thoughts and ideas, we often overlook the silent yet equally dynamic and compelling players in a conversation. Try to envision silence as not merely an absence of words or sounds, but rather view it as a captivating and authoritative force capable of enhancing the dimension and depth of our interactions. So, how does one wield this seemingly paradoxical power? The answer lies in the artful science of silence.

2.1. A Walk through the Sands of Time: Historical Perspective

In an attempt to appreciate the worth of silence, let's embark on a historical exploration. From the monks of the eastern monasteries who practiced silence to cultivate spiritual enlightenment, to the classic rhetoric of Ancient Greece where it was used as a powerful tool in debates, the mindful use of silence has been interwoven with the thread of human communication across generations and cultures. The meaningful pauses within Beethoven's symphonies or the silence before the storm in Shakespeare's plays underline their power and artistry. These carefully curated silences demonstrate how silence, steeped in profound interpretation, can invigorate communication.

2.2. The Anatomy of Silence: A Conceptual Insight

Silence, in the context of communication dialectics, can be delineated into two spectrums: 'Contextual Silence' and 'Intentional Silence'. The former refers to the naturally occurring silence within personal, cultural, and situational contexts. Intentional Silence, on the other hand, deliberately incorporates pauses to either emphasize the spoken word or to let the unvoiced thoughts come forth.

These interpretive pauses in conversation can be analogous to the blank spaces in an art canvas, the silence between the notes in music, or the pause between the actor's lines in theatre. It is within these silences that our minds engage and process communication, calibrate responses, and create space for introspection and connection.

2.3. The Silent Strings: Decoding Body Language and Micro-Expressions

Effective communication goes beyond mere words. Unspoken dynamics greatly influence our narratives. Understanding body language and micro-expressions can vastly increase our perception of these silent messages. For instance, an arched eyebrow might denote surprise, a quick glance might reflect intrigue, and concise nodding can signify acknowledgement. Enhanced perception can simplify complex communication, creating an empathetic interface that encourages open dialogue and understanding.

2.4. The Resounding Echoes of Silence: The Underlying Psychological Aspects

Silence can have profound psychological implications. Our sensorial experience of silence triggers certain neural responses that influence our mental well-being and cognitive processes. For instance, periods of silence can lower stress hormones, stimulate brain growth, and facilitate processing of information.

The psychological aspects of silence are context-dependent. In productive scenarios, silence is a key contributor to concentration, creativity, and insightful thinking. On the other hand, in personal or social dynamics, silence facilitates empathy, tolerance, introspection, and understanding.

Conclusively, harnessing and understanding the artful science of silence is no less than learning an intricate piece of music or a complex work of art. It requires patience, practice, receptivity, and a keen sense of perception. However, once we become adept at this art, the rewards are valuable, from enhanced personal relationships to successful professional interactions. As we delve further into other chapters, we will explore the application of silence against various backdrops, paving the way for a compelling exploration of this incredible and often underrated tool in our communication arsenal.

Chapter 3. Understanding the Power of Pauses

As we embark on an immersive journey into the realm of silence and its role within the sphere of effective communication, one formidable ingredient that comes to light is the humble pause. This chapter seeks to unearth the rich treasure enshrined in pauses, their myriad uses and significance, and how to wield them successfully to enrich one's communicative prowess.

3.1. The Anatomy of a Pause

At first glance, a pause may appear as nothing more than a temporary cessation of speech. However, its simplicity veils a wealth of potentialities. It is during these gaps that listeners can digest the speaker's message, grasping its essence and context. Likewise, the speaker gains a valuable opportunity to gather their thoughts, gauge reactions, or deliver the next point with enhanced impact.

An effective pause is neither too brief and fleeting nor too long and lingering. Striking the balance between the inadequate strain and the excessive stretch is crucial for maintaining the listener's concentration and curiosity. The appropriate length of a pause often hinges on factors such as the speaker's pace, the complexity of the topic, and the cultural and temporal context of the dialogue.

3.2. The Power of Strategic Pausing

Strategic pausing epitomizes a fascinating and resourceful tool in the arsenal of an eloquent communicator. Interlacing speech with well-placed pauses bolsters the speaker's credibility, demonstrating confidence, thoughtfulness, and mastery over the topic at hand.

A passionate speaker often tends to accelerate speech and blur ideas into an unintelligible torrent of words. However, a gentle intervention by a calculated pause contributes to decelerating the tempo, offering both the speaker and the audience a moment for mental respiration. It intensifies the pointed impact, leading the audience along the discussed path with enhanced clarity and comprehension.

3.3. The Silent Amplifier: Pause for Effect

One enchantingly potent utility of a pause lies in its ability to amplify the weight of the spoken words that precede it. Just like how an artist uses negative space to emphasize the subject in a piece of art, a pause helps stress pivotal points in a discourse. Pauses have the silent power to-as one might say-add volume to your speech. By hanging on to the breathless hush following a strong statement, the audience is drawn into a subconscious contemplation of the message, thereby amplifying its impact.

3.4. Pauses and Listener Engagement

Incorporating pauses plays a much-underplayed role in inviting and sustaining listener engagement. A pause is akin to an aural punctuation mark, gently guiding the listeners through the progression of thoughts, just as commas, full stops, and semicolons do in written language. By structuring speech rhythmically, a communicator establishes a mental map in the listener's mind, allowing them to follow the argument or narrative cohesively.

3.5. Embracing the Pause: How to Implement

Mastering the art of pausing is a skill that anyone can nurture with diligent observation and practice. As we converse, we naturally incorporate micro-pauses. Learning to stretch these pauses subtly can usher a transformative effect on one's speech pattern.

One effective technique is known as rhythmic breathing – consciously pairing the intake and release of breath with the ebb and flow of speech. Observing professional orators, seasoned actors, and successful public communicators offers valuable insights into the strategic utilization of pauses.

In the vast universe of communication, the celestial bodies of words are interwoven with the dark matter of silence. This chapter underlines the compelling power behind the seemingly simple act of pausing. When chiseled with wisdom and used with precision, pauses morph into a profound instrument of interaction. They enable a communicator to construct more meaningful, absorbing conversations, thus reinforcing the assertion 'talk less, listen more'. Every pause sown in a conversation promises a bountiful harvest of understanding, empathy, and relatable discourse. Navigate the realm of pauses with the compass of dexterity, and trip the balancing scales of communication to your benefit.

Chapter 4. The Golden Rule: Talk Less, Listen More

In a world that is often overwhelmed with noise and chatter, the importance of silence and listening cannot be overstated. We commence this chapter by examining an important principle referred to as the 'Golden Rule' for effective communication: the art of speaking less and listening more. Aristotle had asserted once that nature has bestowed us with two ears but only one mouth to signify that we ought to listen twice as much as we speak. This principle might sound simple, yet it carries profound implications for personal and professional communication.

4.1. The Golden Rule Defined

In the context of communication, the golden rule: 'Talk Less, Listen More' signifies a balance, with the heavier weighting on the side of listening. It encourages communicators to exercise restraint in their speech, to allow free flow of ideas and viewpoints from others. By listening more, we cultivate an environment that fosters mutual understanding and respect, leading to productive conversations.

Consider the following illustrative scenario: two friends are embroiled in a heated disagreement over a shared misunderstanding. One friend talks incessantly, raising his voice and not allowing the other to express his viewpoint. The conversation ends with increased resentment and a widening chasm of misunderstanding. Conversely, if both friends had adhered to the golden rule, they would have taken turns to express their viewpoints whilst attentively listening to each other. The outcome of this scenario is likely to be a greater understanding of the other's perspective, potentially leading to a resolution of the disagreement.

4.2. Listen Proactively

Just as important as the quantity of listening is the quality. "Active listening", as it's often called, is a conscious effort to truly understand what the speaker is saying, both verbally and non-verbally. This involves not only hearing words but also picking up on non-verbal cues such as tone of voice, body language, and even periods of silence. By honing this empathetic skill, one can unearth underlying thoughts, feelings, and motivations that may not be explicitly communicated.

Perhaps a colleague at work seems unusually quiet during a team meeting. By practicing active listening, one could pick up on subtle differences in their tone of voice or body language, suggesting that something is amiss. Such cues could lead to a private conversation where the concerned colleague feels heard and supported, augmenting team dynamics and trust.

4.3. Balancing Speech and Silence

Indeed, the golden rule is not a strict formula that mandates talking less than 50% of the time. Rather, it propagates a mindset of listening more than speaking. It's about acknowledging that everyone has unique insights and perspectives to offer, which can only be accessed through active listening.

There is a delicate art in balancing speech and silence. It involves assessing the situation and deciphering whether input is necessary or if one should stay silent and listen. Ironically, silence during conversations often carries more weight than words, conveying respect and regard for the speaker's input. Not speaking doesn't necessarily mean passivity; quite the contrary, it shows engagement through mindful listening.

4.4. Efficacious Applications in Professional Settings

The golden rule carries weight and value in all spheres of communication, particularly in professional settings. Business leaders and team members who speak less to listen more foster an environment of trust and collaboration. It encourages innovation as employees who feel heard and valued are more likely to share their ideas and thoughts.

Consider the weekly team meeting scenario, traditionally dominated by managers, leaving little scope for team members to voice their thoughts. By adopting the golden rule, managers can significantly shift this dynamic, turning meetings into platforms for active ideation and discussion, boosting morale, innovation, and productivity.

In conclusion, the Golden Rule: 'Talk Less, Listen More' is not just a principle; it's a mindset and a skill that requires consistent practice and application. The balance of listening more and talking less can be challenging to strike, but its benefits are manifold, ranging from engendering respect and trust to fostering innovation and collaboration. As we journey on towards becoming stronger communicators, the Golden Rule serves as a guiding star, illuminating our path.

Chapter 5. Active Listening: Unlocking Empathetic Communication

Active listening is not merely about being quiet and letting others talk. It's about truly engaging with the speaker, absorbing what is being said, and responding in a way that deepens understanding. This profound level of communication is a tool that can transform relationships, solve problems, and build strong teams. It fosters empathy, showing the speaker that you respect their feelings and point of view. This heightened form of engagement taps into the essence of empathetic communication.

5.1. The Essence of Active Listening

Active listening dictates complete engagement in the dialogue. It entails giving undivided attention to the speaker by shutting down your mental commentary and focusing solely on their words, body language, and emotional expressions. The capacity to actively listen, understand, and respond empathetically is pivotal in building rich, rewarding relationships. The listener should be invested in understanding the speaker's emotions and insights, encouraging them to continue expressing openly.

Active listeners consciously strive to avoid distractions and any premature formulation of responses, instead waiting patiently for the dialogue's natural flow. Attention should be on capturing every nuance of the speaker's message, thereby acknowledging their inherent perspectives and emotions. In doing so, the listener becomes a sounding board that offers subtle, constructive feedback, thereby promoting a thorough exchange of ideas.

5.2. The Empathy Angle

A distinguishing feature between regular listening and active listening is empathy. Empathy, or the ability to understand and share the feelings of others, is the linchpin of active listening. It urges you to step into the shoes of the speaker and see the world from their vantage point. This emotional intelligence bridges the gap between just 'hearing' and truly 'understanding', teaching us to appreciate diverse opinions and respond genuinely.

Tapping into empathy allows us to decipher the emotions ingrained in the speaker's words. At times, the speaker may struggle to articulate their feelings accurately - empathy guides the listener to interpret these unspoken sentiments correctly. This deeper understanding facilitates comprehensive responses, boosting the confidence of the speaker while simultaneously elevating the level of constructive discussion.

5.3. The Key Techniques

There are several techniques which can amplify our ability to listen actively and empathetically.

#Creating a Safe Space Category: The listener should create an environment that's free from distractions, conducive to open discussions and imbued with trust and respect. #Paraphrasing: Demonstrates comprehension by reflecting back the speaker's words in the listener's language, enabling verification of correct understanding. #Undivided Attention: Implies putting aside all devices, thoughts and interruptions, focusing solely on the speaker. #Eye Contact: A consistent gaze shows interest, respect and induces clarity in conversations. #Non-Verbal Cues: Body language like nodding or leaning in, show acknowledgement and encourage speakers to continue. #Feedback: Regular, sensitive feedback endorses the speaker's statements and fosters meaningful conversations. #Open-ended Questions: Encourage speakers to delve deeper into their thoughts and feelings, providing more context and insight. #Emotional Intelligence: Understanding and correctly interpreting the emotional undertones in a speaker's words enhance conversation quality.

Each of these techniques fosters empathetic conversations, facilitating comprehensive understanding and encouraging honest discussions.

5.4. The Barriers to Active Listening

Attaining the level of an active listener is not void of challenges. Common barriers include:

#Inattention: Split attention can impair understanding and frustrate speakers. #Interrupting: Frequent interjections can derail conversations and silence speakers. #Jumping to Conclusions: Premature judgments can cloud our comprehension, leading to inaccuracies. #Mental Filters: Biases can distort our perception, inflicting injustice to the speaker's viewpoint.

Acknowledging these obstacles can hone our listening skills and make us more receptive to different perspectives, thereby fostering more meaningful interactions.

5.5. The Outcomes of Active Listening

Active listening can lead to more authentic, constructive conversations. It builds mutual understanding, encourages openness, and fosters trust. It allows us to build more robust connections with individuals of diverse backgrounds and belief systems.

This practice impacts not only personal interactions but also professional relationships. It helps develop effective leadership, facilitates resolution of conflicts, drives team collaboration and enhances customer relationships.

With its roots firmly grounded in respect and empathy, active listening plays a pivotal role in enriching our network, enhancing our understanding of the world, and placing us on a path toward becoming exceptional communicators. With the above-mentioned techniques and understanding, one can unlock the enormous potential of empathetic communication through active listening.

Chapter 6. Mastering Non-Verbal Communication

Mastering non-verbal communication involves more than understanding the messages we unconsciously send through body language and facial expressions; it's about establishing a connection without uttering a single word. It's an intricate and complex skill, woven into the fabric of our daily lives as human beings - a universal language spoken by all, but mastered by few. In the following sections, you'll be introduced to the different elements of non-verbal communication and learn how to use them effectively to resonate with others on a deeper, more meaningful level.

6.1. The Pillars of Non-Verbal Communication

Non-verbal communication is built upon five main pillars: body language, facial expression, tone and pitch of voice, physical touch, and personal space. Body language is essentially our gestures, posture, and movement - the way we move our bodies, which often express more than our verbiage. Facial expression is the physical manifestation of our emotions and thoughts. It's said that over 90% of human emotional expression takes place through our faces.

The tone and pitch of our voice can alter the meaning of our words entirely, adding layers of complexity to our verbal communication. Physical touch, while often overlooked, is an integral player in the realm of non-verbal communication. From a simple pat on the back to a comforting hug, physical touch can express a wide range of emotions.

Personal space, finally, pertains to the proximity between you and the person you're interacting with. It's a nonverbal marker of intimacy, familiarity, and personal comfort levels. By understanding and respecting these five pillars, we can enhance our ability to communicate effectively without using words.

6.2. Decoding Facial Expressions

Facial expressions are an efficient way for humans to express emotions without words. From the furrowing of eyebrows in confusion to the widening of eyes in surprise or fear, our faces are continually speaking volumes. It's also one of the most universal aspects of non-verbal communication, with certain expressions understood by all cultures.

Recognizing and correctly interpreting facial expressions is a crucial step towards mastering the art of non-verbal communication. However, it's equally essential to understand that individuals may display emotions differently based on their personal or cultural norms. As such, careful attention and cultural sensitivity are paramount.

6.3. Reading Body Language

The analysis of body language, or kinesics, is a fundamental tool for understanding non-verbal communication. Psychologists suggest we communicate more information using our body than we do verbally. Posture, gestures, body movements, or even the way we stand can convey a hidden narrative or amplify the messages spoken aloud.

For instance, crossed arms might imply defensiveness, while a relaxed posture may indicate openness or comfort. However, these interpretations are not universal. Therefore, it's crucial to consider the context, cultural background, and personal habits when interpreting body language.

6.4. Grasping Paralanguage

Paralanguage refers to vocal communication cues separate from language. It includes pitch, volume, rate of speech, vocal quality, and intonation, among others. Even silent phenomena like pauses or sighs fall under paralanguage. While words express the 'what' in communication, paralanguage expresses the 'how'. In mastering nonverbal communication, being alert and responsive to these vocal signs can add depth to our understanding of others' intentions and emotions.

6.5. Comprehending Touch

The language of touch, or haptics, is one of the most personal forms of nonverbal communication. A firm handshake, a friendly pat, a constrictive hug - each carries with it a language of its own. While powerful, touch can also be misunderstood due to cultural or personal preferences. It's crucial to consider boundaries and comfort levels while using touch as a means of communication.

6.6. Respecting Personal Space

Lastly, understanding the significance of space, or proxemics, is an integral part of nonverbal communication. The distance we maintain during conversations can reveal relationship dynamics or indicate the level of comfort or discomfort. It differs from culture to culture and from person to person. Respecting personal space is an essential aspect of effective non-verbal communication.

In bringing together a detailed understanding of these elements, mastering non-verbal communication can greatly enhance the richness and depth of our interactions. The study and practice of non-verbal communication are vast fields ripe for ongoing exploration. Invested effort here not only ensures better communication but also encourages nurturing relationships built on understanding, empathy, and respect.

Chapter 7. The Impact of Silence in Difficult Conversations

Conversations of a difficult nature – be it a challenging negotiation, a disagreement with a peer, or a potentially distressing personal discussion – are often ones that are fraught with heightened emotions and a lack of understanding. In such circumstances, the conventional wisdom seems to suggest a need for more words, more explanations, more reasoning in an attempt to bridge misunderstanding. However, this approach can at times lead to conversational quicksand - the more you struggle, the deeper you sink. Instead, an exploration of the strategic usage of silence can yield more effective results, allowing you to navigate these tricky waters with a newfound adeptness.

7.1. The Power of Silence in Difficult Conversations

The effective use of silence is an advanced communication strategy in difficult conversations. Used correctly, it has the potential to diffuse tense situations, providing the space needed for emotions to subside and for clearer thought processes to take place. A pause can serve as a psychological 'reset', offering individuals involved in the conversation a chance to recalibrate, reassess their positions, and respond instead of reacting.

Often overlooked is the fact that silence gives signification to our words; the pauses between our thoughts emphasizing them, allowing for a deeper penetration of our arguments into the minds of our counterpart. This, in essence, is the latent power of silence – a tool so subtle, yet so impactful.

7.2. The Impact of Silence: A Scientific Perspective

Neuroscientific research corroborates the assertion that silence in conversation can be used as a mechanism to promote comprehension and nurture empathy. According to a study in the journal "Neuron", silence immediately following a piece of information allows it to be processed and committed to memory more effectively.

Moreover, a calm silence can decrease the production of cortisol, commonly known as the 'stress hormone'. This has the dual effect of reducing agitation and increasing clarity of thought, leading to a more principled dialogue rather than an emotionally charged argument. Integrating these silent pauses in conversations can yield significant positive results, reducing the propensity for misunderstandings and increasing the likelihood of reaching an amicable resolution.

7.3. Practicing the Pause: The Power of Delayed Response

Adopting silence into your conversation strategy involves more than merely abstaining from words. A key technique is the art of 'delayed response', where one consciously takes time to process the information, formulate a coherent viewpoint, and then respond. This might seem awkward initially, possibly being perceived as non-attentiveness or even rudeness. But with conscientious application, it soon becomes a sign of respect, indicative of careful consideration being given to the words spoken.

A delayed response also constructs space for consideration of the other individual's perspective. In effect, you are communicating without speaking – conveying that you recognize the validity of their viewpoint, and deem it worthy of reflection before responding.

7.4. Final Thoughts

The art of employing silence in difficult conversations is not about weaponizing quietude, but rather it's about utilizing it as a legitimate and valuable communication tool. Understanding its role and impact is the first step in learning to harness it effectively. While the practice of implementing strategic silence may seem unnatural at first, with patience and persistence, it can become a powerful component of your communication toolkit, allowing for more effective and empathic dialogues in situations that demand a heightened level of understanding and sensitivity.

In conclusion, difficult conversations need not be a battleground of words, for silence, wielded adeptly, can serve as a bridge, enabling understanding and mutual respect. With this newfound understanding of the impact of silence in difficult conversations, you are equipped to transform the way you communicate. Your journey towards becoming a better listener and communicator has only just begun!

Chapter 8. Harnessing Silence for Persuasion and Influence

The process of persuasion is akin to a fine dance, tracing a delicate balance between convincing arguments and receptivity. Most conversations, especially in persuasive contexts, tend to prioritize talking and asserting one's ideas. Predominantly, these interactions focus on applying assertive language, logical reasoning, and emotional pleas to influence or change someone else's mindsets, decisions, or actions. While these established tactics do have their value, one often-overlooked tool is silence. Borrowing from the adage that silence is golden, we explore the unspoken potency it holds in persuasive dynamics.

8.1. The Enigma of Silence in Persuasion

Silence, in its quintessential form, is a lack of sound or speech. When incorporated into conversations and arguments, however, it evolves into a far more nuanced communicative instrument. Applied as a strategic tool, silence possesses the subtle power to shape the course and outcome of a persuasive interaction.

When wielded correctly, silence creates spaces in dialogue that amplify the weight of the words preceding them. This amplification stems from the exchange dynamics that exist within a conversation. Often, interlocutors perceive silence as a cue for them to talk, which is precisely why it's a tool of influence. Through a well-placed pause, an individual can subtly prompt the other to continue speaking, consequently driving the conversation while listening more and speaking less.

Additionally, silence provides respite from the rapid interchange of ideas, providing an opportunity for individuals to process information and form their responses. This 'thinking window' can significantly change the course of persuasive interactions.

8.2. Leveraging Silence as an Active Construct

While silence is naturally thought of as a passive force - a lack, an absence, a non-doing - in the sphere of communication dynamics, it becomes an active construct. Silence effects a transition from a traditional 'talk-listen' model to a more balanced, equally participatory 'listen-talk-listen' model. This active use of silence brings forth its dual ability: enabling one to glean more substantial information from their counterpart and affording a more considered, impactful verbal response.

To harness this power effectively, several techniques can be employed. The first of these is the use of reflective silence. This is a strategic pause following the other party's statements, creating a non-verbal indication that the information provided is being considered. The pause indicates respect for the speaker's comments, and the resultant silence often compels them to elaborate further, providing additional valuable information.

The second technique is the use of probing silence. This method is especially effective in negotiation settings. When compared to direct questioning, a well-placed silence can unearth more in-depth and thoughtful responses. The third technique is the use of reciprocal silence, where silence is used to match the other party's non-verbals, creating a rapport and encouraging openness.

8.3. The Risks and Rewards of Silence

However, like any tool, silence doesn't come without its share of risks. Using pauses too frequently or at inappropriate times can cause disconnection or confusion. Therefore, it is vital to read the situation correctly and judge when and where to insert silence for maximum impact.

Despite these potential challenges, the rewards of effectively using silence are substantial. The silent interludes can give you the upper hand in guiding the conversation without appearing to dominate it. It allows persuasion to occur subtly and naturally, resulting in a more genuine influence dynamic. This authenticity of influence catalyzes stronger relationships, paves the way for successful outcomes, and enhances the overall communication experience

8.4. Silence and the Age of Digital Communication

In the digital age, the application of silence has also morphed. In written communications, silence manifests in the form of thoughtful pauses, deliberate delays in response, or even strategic withholding of immediate responses. This nuanced use of silence can be an equally persuasive tool in digital communication platforms.

In conclusion, silence is not merely an absence of words but a strategic tool equipped to tilt the scales of influence. From drawing out deeper insights to heightening emotional impact, silence allows us to exercise persuasion subtly and effectively. Consequently, silence, when harnessed correctly, enhances our ability to connect, empathize, and influence others, fortifying the pillars of effective communication.

Chapter 9. The Echo of Silence in Digital Communication

As we move further into the realm of the digital age, communication, interestingly enough, has become increasingly synonymous with the act of silent messaging. Text messages, emails, even social media posts perhaps constitute the majority of communication conducted by the average individual on a daily, if not hourly, basis. This transitional shift in the modality of communication offers the opportunity to delve deeper into the essence of silent communication, and more specifically, the profound echo of silence within the sphere of digital correspondence.

9.1. The Silent Nuances of Digital Communication

Digital communication serves as a double-edged sword. On one hand, the absence of traditional face-to-face interaction eliminates the multifaceted stimuli involved in physical conversation, such as tone, body language, and facial expressions, turning communication into a simplified and immediate exercise. On the contrary, the lack of these cues makes understanding the intent or sentiment behind a message more challenging.

Fortuitously, we have at our disposal a set of tools within the sphere of text-based digital dialogue that can help infer tone and emotion, including emoticons, gifs, and deliberate text formatting. Even so, the question arises: How does silence reverberate in such a setting? What does a delayed response imply? How does the absence of an emoji or a subdued 'LOL' transform the interpretation of a message?

The answers to these questions are complex, multifaceted, and utterly engrossing, carrying massive implications for our ongoing negotiation and navigation of our digital social landscape.

9.2. Silence as a Digital Artifact

Within the framework of a digital conversation, silence emerges as an artifact – a thing left behind that mimics its usage in physical dialogue. It is very much possible to 'hear' silence, and its subtleties vary based on the scenario. For instance, an extended gap between messages may resonate as an irritated silence or may reflect the sender's preoccupation with another matter. Similarly, the conspicuous absence of a response to a particular query fuels various interpretations.

The receiver is left to decipher these silences, often leading to speculation and assumptions. The art of reading and interpreting these silent intervals, or the absence of verbal content, when combined with contextualizing surrounding text is a skill that behooves adaption in the digital age.

9.3. Digital Silence: A Tool for Strategic Communication

Correspondingly, silence can be employed within the digital realm as a strategic mechanism. A delayed response can exhibit disinterest, or it can be a stalling tactic, giving the sender more time to think before responding. Moreover, deciding not to use an emoji or limiting the use of enthusiastic punctuation can create a more serious or professional tone.

Of course, such calculated employment of silence demands consideration of the potential effects on the recipients. Understanding how various elements of digital silence will be decoded by your recipient, as well as the ultimate objective of the communication, are crucial considerations in designing your digital discourse.

9.4. Towards Mindful Digital Silence

The dynamics of digital conversation mirror those of in-person interaction, where strategic use of silence can be used to convey a message. Silence in digital communication is very much a conscious act, one that can have a profound effect on shaping interactions and relationships.

Fully grasping the concept of digital silence would mean examining our personal communication habits, whether it's the needless overuse of emojis or 'lol's, the downtime between replies, or the preferred way of crafting personal or professional digital messages.

Moreover, we have to be mindful of how others interpret our digital silence and the different forms it assumes. Every silent cue in our digital discourse carries the potential to be a meaningful communication tool, requiring mindfulness, intention, and skillful execution.

In the ever-evolving realm of digital correspondence, it is imperative to keep refining one's sense of digital dynamics, adjusting and adapting as the patterns of communication continue to shift beneath our fingertips. Understanding the echo of silence in digital communication opens a new door in the realm of silent communication, enabling us to connect more meaningfully in the virtual world, transcending the limits of physicality and time.

Every delayed response, every subdued 'lol,' every strategically employed emoji, or the lack thereof, becomes a fundamental component, enhancing our overarching comprehension of digital discourse. The power of silence is certainly not confined to the realm of audio perception; it resides in every aspect of our communication and can transform our digital interactions to deliver enhanced understanding and stronger connectivity.

Chapter 10. Silence and Leadership: An Unforeseen Connection

The whispers of silence, often overlooked in the cacophony of leadership dialogues, surprisingly, hold an immense power to shape and influence. This chapter, through comprehensive insights, enlightening examples, and empirical evidence, will underscore the rather unforeseen and understated connection between silence and leadership.

10.1. The Power of Silent Leadership

A leader is traditionally perceived as someone who communicates assertively, guiding, and directing others through fluent speeches and expressive body language. However, much of the essence of true leadership lies in 'silent leadership.' Silent leadership refers to the influential power and control demonstrated, not through words or loud pronouncements, but the grandeur of silence, active listening, and strategic communication breaks.

There is a unique credibility and authority in leaders who listen more and speak less. These leaders let their actions speak louder than their words, making lasting impacts on team dynamics and organizational culture. Their silent leadership builds a transformative environment of mutual respect, empathy, and trust, fostering more innovative ideas and effective problem-solving.

Furthermore, silent leadership encourages diverse voices to emerge and be heard. This inclusion of ideas fosters team solidarity and promotes a culture of collaboration and innovation.Various studies corroborate that silent leadership cultivates an environment of psychological safety, where team members feel secure to freely express their views and opinions.

10.2. Silence: A Strategic Tool

Leadership communication is not merely about commanding others; it extends to discerning and comprehending the unsaid expressions, sentiments, and concerns. To hone this skill, leaders need to embrace the power of silence as their strategic tool.

Leaders who listen more than they speak engender a sense of value, trust, and respect among their team members. This silence encourages a dynamic, two-way communication channel where ideas are freely exchanged, heard, and appreciated. Leaders can strategically employ silence during negotiations, in making important decisions, or when managing conflicts. A well-timed pause can carry more weight than any stinging argument or passionate speech.

This strategy of silence allows leaders to digest the information, give it thoughtful consideration, and respond rationally rather than impulsively. In return, this encourages team members to fill in the silence with their thoughts, leading to open-ended conversations that spark innovation and progress.

10.3. Leaders Who Mastered the Art of Silence

Historical and contemporary figures exemplify the potent connection between leadership and silence. Leaders like Mahatma Gandhi and Nelson Mandela, despite their contrasting leadership styles, were known for their uncanny ability to wield silence as a potent leadership tool. They strategically used silence to ponder, reflect, and strategically plan their actions during times of adversity and resistance.

Within corporate settings, introverted leaders such as Bill Gates and Warren Buffett are seen as master communicators who leverage the power of silence. Despite their quiet demeanor, these leaders have made remarkable impacts on their organizations, demonstrating that silence doesn't imply absence; instead, it can underpin presence, power, and influence.

10.4. Crafting Silence into Your Leadership Style

Incorporating silence into leadership styles can seem daunting. It goes against the conventional definition of a leader as an assertive, dynamic, and vocal presence. However, redefining leadership to include the subtleties of silent communication can dramatically enhance leadership effectiveness.

Silent Listening: Active and empathic listening is one of the most advanced skills a leader can master. It fosters deeper relationships, aids in resolving conflicts, and facilitates better decision-making. Leaders should intentionally set aside time to listen and engage with their team members, enabling them to voice their concerns, share their ideas and insights.

Silent Reflection: Silence provides leaders with the time and space for reflection. During these periods, leaders can introspect, gain clarity on issues, think strategically, and plan the future course of action. Regular reflections embedded in silence can lead to profound insights and thoughtfully crafted decisions.

Silent Presence: Often, leaders feel the burden to fill every silence or gap in conversations. However, the intentional practice of maintaining silent presence communicates calm, control, and respect. A leader's silence can convey deep understanding and empathy, providing comfort and assurance in times of uncertainty.

Embracing silence doesn't imply leaders should remain quiet or lose their voice. Instead, it underscores the importance of balancing verbal and non-verbal communication strategically. For all aspiring to be exceptional leaders, this chapter forms a stepping stone in acknowledging the power of silence and nimble quietude, enhancing their capacity to lead, inspire, and influence.

Chapter 11. Infusing Silence into Everyday Communication for Lasting Impact

The closing chapter of this enlightening exploration into the world of silent communication aims to cement our understanding of how we may infuse silence into our everyday exchanges and make a lasting impact on our acquaintances.

11.1. The Nuances of Silent Communication

The concept of 'communication' generally invokes images of words, sounds, gestures, and symbols—everything but silence. Yet, our earlier discussions have illuminated how silence can be an equally expressive tool for communication. Strategically punctuating your verbal or written messages with silent pauses can open doors to deeper comprehension and more effective conveyance of your intentions.

11.2. The Power of Pauses - Reigniting the Flame

While pauses are often considered negative spaces in a conversation, they can indeed be potent enablers when it comes to stress management, decision-making, and emotion control. A well-timed pause allows us to gather scattered thoughts, regain control, and steer a conversation in our intended direction.

This is something we can practice in everyday communication. Start by training yourself to count silently before reacting to emotions during a conversation. Gradually, you will notice that this extra time lets you reflect and respond more empathetically, while potentially averting heated disputes. Taking a pause could also give you the well-needed breather to reconsider critical decisions, helping you make a more informed choice.

11.3. Active Listening - Silent Yet Engaged

We have already discussed extensively how silence and attentive, active listening go hand-in-hand. However, understanding how to infuse this into everyday communication might be more challenging than one would assume.

Active listening goes beyond the act of 'listening' itself - it involves focusing on the speaker and understanding their words, emotions, and perspectives. To practice active listening, try engaging in silence when someone else is talking, instead of formulating your response. Show your engagement through non-verbal cues, like nodding or maintaining eye contact, that convey your attention without disrupting the speaker.

"Listening is an attitude of the heart, a genuine desire to be with another which both attracts and heals." - L. J. Isham

11.4. Non-Verbal Communication - Beyond Words

Applying silence to non-verbal communication implies using body movements, facial expressions, and touch more effectively to put across your intentions or convey empathy. By focusing on improving your body language, you can communicate your enthusiasm, respect, agreement, or disagreement without uttering a single word.

Positive non-verbal cues, like a smile, an open posture, or an empathetic pat on the back, can ease tension and foster a more open and honest conversation. Avoiding negative gestures like crossing arms or appearing distracted not only prevents misinterpretations but also builds trust and strengthens relationships.

11.5. Difficult Conversations and the Use of Silence

Each of us, at some point, have faced uncomfortable or difficult conversations. Silence can be a recourse during such times. It not only indicates your willingness to listen but also showcases your patience and consideration for the other person's perspective. Moreover, delayed reactions or responses can often deescalate a potentially explosive situation, ensuring communication stays civil and productive.

11.6. Harnessing Silence for Personal Influence

Silence can be a powerful persuader. The strategic use of silent moments can invoke thought, impart seriousness, or establish authority. In persuasion, silence gives the other participant time to process your argument, thus potentiate agreeability. Experimenting with silent communication in everyday scenarios, like proposing ideas at work or negotiating with a vendor, can help you embark the journey towards becoming a more influential communicator.

11.7. Digital Communication

In the digital age, the echoes of silence resonate in ways previously unimagined. Online, silence can be manifested in thoughtful pauses before responding to an email, allowing for strategic thought formulation or diffusing tension. Conversely, electronic silence can exemplify a digital detox, in the spirit of self-care, or even a silent protest against cyberbullying or digital oversharing.

11.8. Silence and Leadership: Bring it Together

Leadership requires strategic communication—knowing what, when, and how to speak. But equally important is knowing when to remain silent. Silence creates an atmosphere of respect, encourages team members to voice their views, and promotes a democratic leadership style, which makes for a healthier organisational culture.

11.9. The Future of Silence in Everyday Communication

Throwing light on the future of silence in everyday communication highlights the urgency to move beyond traditional perceptions and acknowledge silence as a vital communication tool. This shift will demand cultural acceptance and personal practice.

In summary, regularly infusing silence into our interactions can remarkably elevate our skills as communicators. Understanding its potential and mastering its use constitutes the final goal in our journey towards more enriching and satisfying communication experiences. End the chatter, embrace the silence, and watch as your communication skills transform from ordinary to extraordinary!

This chapter should imbue you with the knowledge to employ silence as a potent tool in daily communication, letting you embark on a lifelong journey towards mastering silent communication. Remember, silence is not the absence of communication, but an integral part of it. Infuse silence and make a lasting impact!